THE
Archive Photographs
SERIES

GLOSSOP

Miles Francis Fitzalan Howard, seventeenth Duke of Norfolk, fourth Baron Howard of Glossop. His predecessors played a large part in the development of the modern Glossop by planning the centre of the town around Norfolk Square, building the Town Hall, Market Hall and railway station, and promoting the turnpike road - the Snake Pass - to Sheffield.

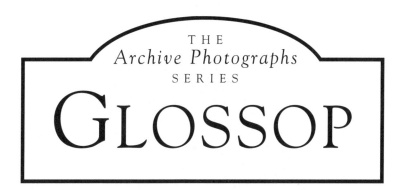

THE
Archive Photographs
SERIES

GLOSSOP

Compiled by
Edith Bennett

CHALFORD

First published 1997
Copyright © Edith Bennett, 1997

The Chalford Publishing Company
St Mary's Mill, Chalford,
Stroud, Gloucestershire, GL6 8NX

ISBN 0 7524 1009 1

Typesetting and origination by
The Chalford Publishing Company
Printed in Great Britain by
Bailey Print, Dursley, Gloucestershire

Dedication
To my husband, Jim

Contents

Acknowledgements   6

Introduction   7

1.   Shops, Streets and Roads   9

2.   Buildings   33

3.   Transport   51

4.   Working Life   63

5.   The Wood Family   77

6.   Churches and Chapels   89

7.   Leisure Activities   105

8.   Events and Celebrations   115

A panoramic view over the Glossop countryside, showing the Glossop skyline.

Acknowledgements

All the photographs in this book belonged to my late husband, Jim Bennett. His hobby was building up a large collection of photographs of Glossop as it was in the past, reproduced from original photographs, newspaper photographs and family albums. He built up a library of pictures which illustrated life in Glossop from the time the camera was invented in the 1860s. I decided to publish a book of these photographs in memory of Jim and I should like to express my thanks to the countless people who gave or loaned their original photographs to him. I should also like to thank Peggy Davies, manager of Glossop Heritage Centre, who has written and typed the captions.

Edith Bennett
1997

Introduction

Glossop is a town with a long and historic past. The valley system was formed by the Ice Age carving the hills and gouging out the deep valleys. About 4,000 BC, the trees on the tops of the moors rotted and died, leaving a thick layer of peat; today the tops of the moors are covered with heather and bracken. Early Man hunted in this valley, leaving behind his arrow heads and scrapers to be found centuries later.

The Romans came to Glossopdale in about 79 AD when they built their fort at Melandra, but by 140 AD, the Roman garrison was needed elsewhere and the fort was abandoned. Between 410 AD and 850 AD, waves of invaders came from North Germany. These Angles made their first settlement here, and one of these Anglians settlers was called 'Glott', who tried to scratch a living where the forest line in the valley bottom met the moor line at about 600 feet. This valley was known as Glott's valley, but the Anglo-Saxon word for valley was 'Hop', so the place became spoken of as 'Glott's Hop', from which the name Glossop was derived.

At the time of Domesday in 1086, there were ten settlements in what later became the Manor of Glossop. Hadfield, Padfield, Dinting and Charlesworth were all mentioned in Domesday Book. This part of the Royal Forest was governed by the son of William the Conqueror and later, by the Abbot of Basingwerke in 1157. Perhaps this period saw a church built in Glossop. After the dissolution of the monasteries by Henry VIII, the Glossop lands were given to the Talbot Earls of Shrewsbury, the most successful northern family of Tudor England. The Earl's youngest daughter married Thomas Howard in 1606 and part of her dowry was the Glossopdale Estate, which in this way passed into the Howard family, who were to remain lords of the manor until 1926. The original name of the present town was 'Howardtown', named after the Howard family. Over 100 houses built in the seventeenth century still survive today.

At this time the domestic spinning wheel and the hand loom were increasingly used in the growing cottage industry, first in wool and later in cotton. In 1700 the population increased and the development of the textile industry led to the expansion of the town. An ample supply of fast running water ensured that Glossop - conveniently near Manchester - became one of the centres of the emerging cotton industry. The new techniques of Crompton and Arkwright were sufficiently accessible to the new, small mill owners of Glossop to sustain development, and there was rapid growth between 1785 and 1831, when forty-six mills were built along the several streams which provided them with power.

Rows and rows of stone terraced houses were built around the town to house the army of cotton workers. The development of steam power led to the growth of individual mills and by the mid nineteenth century, Glossop was a town of few but enormous mills. The population grew six times in half a century and thus the sizeable Glossop we know today was created. The largest mill was the Howardtown Mill, owned by the Wood family; the second largest mill was Wren Nest Mill, managed by Francis Sumner.

The new turnpike roads crossing each other in the centre of the town became a convenient focus for industry and housing development. The ancient village of Glossop after twelve centuries - seven of them as an administrative centre - had gone into retirement as 'Old Glossop'.

The twelfth Duke of Norfolk built the Town Hall in 1837, into which the organs of local government soon moved, and the thirteenth Duke of Norfolk built the Market Hall in 1844 and the railway station in 1847, having been instrumental in building the railway branch line into Glossop from the main Manchester to Sheffield line, which by-passed the town.

Edward Partington's rise in the paper manufacturing industry brought him to Glossop in 1873 and he was the largest of Glossop's personalities, becoming Baron Doverdale in 1917, outranking the later baronetcies of Sir John Hill-Wood in 1918, and Sir Samuel Hill-Wood in 1921. In 1866 the town was granted a Royal Borough Charter and Francis Sumner was the first mayor. Upon the formation of the Borough, many fine buildings were built and donated to the town by private benefactors. Another donation in Jubilee year, 1887, was the opening of Howard Park, provided by the Wood family with the swimming pool and the local hospital donated by the same family.

Through lack of investment and the loss of overseas markets, Glossop mills finally closed down in the 1950s and '60s and the Partington paper mills closed in 1963. In 1925 a larger historical connection was broken. The Howards, after 300 years of dominance in the dale, sold all the Glossopdale Estates and Glossop Hall. The Hall was demolished in 1956 and the grounds were turned into Manor Park by the Glossop Borough Council. The great industrialists had already left the dale before 1925.

With the large, local industries gone, Glossop changed its role. The town now has a few local industries and they are on a much smaller scale than the large cotton industry, employing fewer people, and Glossop Borough became part of the larger High Peak Borough when local government was reorganised. Now, Glossop has become a dormitory town for Manchester yet remains essentially unchanged in lay out and character. The Town Hall is still there in Norfolk Square, with its familiar clock tower, and the High Street, with its shops and trees, remains little changed. The magnificent moorlands of the Peak National Park surround the valley, reminding everyone of those early settlers who found the dale attractive, just as today, new settlers are attracted to make their home in this ancient township in the Southern Pennines.

Peggy Davies
1997

One
Shops, Streets and Roads

High Street West, Glossop, with a Glossop tram. People could travel three miles to Hadfield for one old penny. High Street Wesley Chapel is clearly shown; it opened in 1844 and was one of the largest chapels in Glossop.

TOWN HALL

Norfolk Square, set out with lawns and the original diagonal paths before the trees were planted. Also evident is the Town Hall, with its familiar clock tower and adjacent shops, their windows bulging with goods for sale.

T.P. Hunter's grocers shop in High Street West. No one seems to mind the bacon and hams hanging outside the shop. With freshly combed hair and clean aprons, staff pose for the photographer. Woolworth's shop now occupies this site next to the Town Hall.

10

Victoria Street, Glossop, with the tram lines clearly visible and Littlemoor Sunday School tower on the right. The horse probably belonged to the paper mill of Olive & Partington and was used for fetching the wood logs from the station to the mill.

Another view of Victoria Street, looking in the opposite direction, with the spire of St James's Church, Whitfield, silhouetted in the gloomy smog. This smog, emitted from the numerous mill chimneys, used to hang over Glossop.

High Street West, Glossop.

Looking up High Street West around 1908, the main features being the support poles carrying the tram power cables, and the sun shades over the shop windows.

The Glossop tram passing the Town Hall around 1915; the local boys are attracted to the photographer. On the right are the windows of Boots the chemist, packed full of pills and potions.

Glossop was blessed with a large number of Co-operative Society stores, easily recognisable by their standard building style. These shops were well known for their window displays of tinned cans in pyramids. This store was situated in Pikes Lane, Whitfield.

A similar store in Manor Park Road, near its junction with High Street East. All the Co-operative stores gradually closed, to be concentrated in the society's own self-service supermarket near to the railway station in the centre of town.

Phillip Howard Road in Glossop, named after the Hon Phillip Howard, son of Francis Howard, second Baron Howard of Glossop; he died in the First World War and his name is on the Glossop War Memorial. The road was set out as a boulevard with trees, lawns and flower beds. The Howardtown Mill, belonging to the Wood family, can be seen in the background.

A different kind of street, showing the homes of the cotton workers. This is Edward Street, Glossop, decorated for the visit of the Glossop Cotton Queen, Frances Lockett, in 1930. The queens were chosen from different districts of the cotton mills in the North West. On all local grand occasions Bernard Street and Edward Street were always the most highly decorated streets in Glossop.

14

Another decorated street in Glossop, this time to celebrate Queen Victoria's Jubilee. The photograph shows High Street East shops where the Howard Arms is just around the corner.

The pawnbrokers shop in High Street West, next door to the Town Hall. This was a popular shop with the unemployed cotton workers when times were bad.

Slatelands Road, Glossop, when there were no traffic problems, *c.* 1910.

The junction of Hall Street (Manor Park Road) and High Street East, *c.* 1910. The children in the photograph are clustered around the drinking fountain which was erected by the Hon Mrs John Wood, from Whitfield House, Glossop.

John Connor and his wife, standing at the door of his general store at the bottom of High Street West, just above the Grapes Inn, *c*. 1905.

Dinting Lane, Glossop, with the gas lamp and the cobblestones around 1914. The man in the foreground is probably carrying coal in the bucket for his fire.

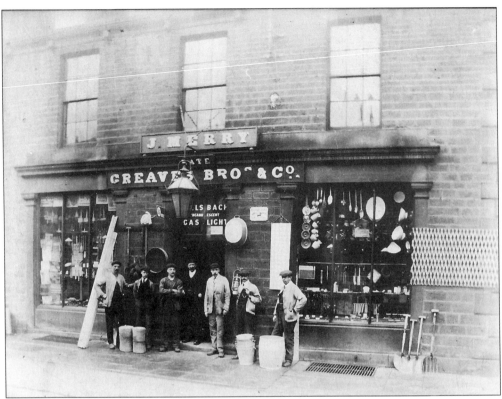

A typical hardware store, *c.* 1919. This one belonged to Mr Merry in High Street East, opposite the Manor Inn. He was a general ironmonger, a tinplate worker and gas and water fitter.

The bakers van outside Platt's the bakers in Shrewsbury Street, Glossop. There is still a bakers establishment there today.

Kiln Lane, Hadfield, in 1904, with the Mason Arms public house on the right. This scene is not very different from today except for the fashions, the shop and the gas street lamp.

Bank Street, Hadfield, with the large Bank Street Chapel at the top of the hill, *c.* 1910.

Top of Station Road, Hadfield, at the bus terminus with one of the early buses, with the open top, which succeeded the trams in 1926. The Hadfield Library on the left was the gift of Mr Platt, a local cotton mill owner, to the people of Hadfield.

Hadfield Road and Old Hall Square in 1911. The building on the right was St Andrew's Church vicarage for many years. The three-storeyed houses lower down the road were weavers' cottages. The women and children spun the cotton on the ground floor whilst the man of the house was the weaver on the top floor.

Station Road, Hadfield, showing the Hadfield Post Office on its original site in the early 1900s.

Hadfield, showing the rows and rows of stone terraced cottages built to house hundreds of mill workers, c. 1900. In the centre of the photograph is the prominent Methodist Chapel on Bank Street and to the right is St Andrews's C of E Church. Both of these places of worship attracted the patronage of the people who owned the mills which employed most of the Hadfield workers.

Miss Shaw, standing at the door of her sweet shop in Hadfield Road, Hadfield in the 1890s. This shop was very popular with the young pupils who attended the Methodist School across the road and who often spent their pennies on sweets instead of reading, writing and arithmetic.

Levi Lee, Sunday School Superintendent at St Andrew's Church, Hadfield, owned this shop in Hadfield Road. It was a typical grocers corner shop of the 1890s.

The barbers shop, belonging to E. Bouchey, stood at the corner of Bankbottom and Waterside in Hadfield around 1880. The long white aprons worn by staff were the uniform of the day in the shops.

Mr Lee had a fish and chip shop in Hadfield, selling wet fish as well as cooked fish. He is wearing clogs on his feet, the customary footwear of the time.

Cottage Lane, Gamesley, a hamlet but still part of Glossop. It is interesting to see that the lane does not even have cobblestones; it is a dirt road, with dirt footpaths and just one flagstone at the gate of each house. In 1905 the children are bewitched by the cameraman, the boys with their best Sunday collars and the girls with their hats.

Glossop Road, Charlesworth, in about 1910, showing the popular transport of the day.

Town Lane, Charlesworth. The gas lamp was replaced by the village war memorial.

Another view of Town Lane around 1920, with two shire horses pulling the carts - the only type of transport for the village.

The houses in Glossop Road, Charlesworth, showing the hazards of horse transport: piles of manure in the road.

A rural scene at Woodseats Lane, Charlesworth. This lane went from the main turnpike road from Marple to Glossop, and was built in 1803. It was used by the many cotton workers who lived in Charlesworth but who worked at the cotton mills in Broadbottom, on the River Etherow.

The main turnpike road from Manchester to Sheffield at Tintwistle, which like Glossop is now under the same local authority. This road was built in 1788 when stagecoaches were the means of transport. At the time of this photograph, people were able to walk in the middle of the road and share it with the horse and cart. Today it is snarled up with heavy traffic all day long.

This was, and still is known as 'New Road', Tintwistle. This road joins Hadfield with Tintwistle and with the main turnpike road, which can be seen at the top. The Church Inn, on the main road, was a coaching inn where stage coaches used to call to change horses before their long journey over the moors to Sheffield.

The bridge over Bray Clough, which provided the water to power the old woollen mill seen in the middle of the photograph. This mill was working in 1790 before the cotton mills were built.

A moorland road traversing the hills from Glossop to Woodhead and on to Sheffield. The photograph shows the wild countryside which surrounds Glossop and the roads have to twist and turn to negotiate the contours of the hills. This particular bend in the road is known locally as 'Devil's Elbow'.

Another moorland road going southward from Glossop towards Hayfield and Buxton. The photograph shows one of the approach footpaths to the great plateau of Kinder Scout, rising to over 2,000 feet on the right.

One of the most famous Pennine Passes, the notorious Snake Pass outside Glossop, with an early motor car negotiating a tight bend. The road 'snakes' its way over the moors but its name is not based on this, but rather on the serpent which appears on the coat of arms of the Duke of Devonshire, on whose land the road was built.

The Manchester Road (4)

Another view of the spectacular Snake Pass carrying the road from Manchester over the rugged moors to Sheffield. The road passes through Glossop and then leaves the houses behind to become one of the most exposed and spectacular highways in the country. It was the last turnpike road to be built in Glossop in 1821. This photograph shows the Hurst Brook flowing down the rocky gorge to Glossop, where it joins first the Shelf Brook and then the River Etherow, a tributary of the River Mersey.

This view shows the other side of the Snake Pass and the beautiful scenery of the Woodland Valley with the start of another river system flowing to the east. The river is the River Ashop and in the 1930s the river was dammed to make the Ladybower Reservoir, which provides water for the city of Sheffield. The hills on the left are the eastern approach hills to Kinder Scout.

A panoramic view of Glossop from the Snake Pass, showing the open fields which eventually became Glossop Golf Club.

One of the main roads from Manchester to Glossop. The road had to negotiate the hills around the town and this meant a deep cutting through the hard rock, which is clearly visible in the photograph. In the early days people could walk in the middle of the road but today it is full of heavy traffic. The road to Mottram is always referred to as the Deep Cutting.

Cuthbert's tobacconist shop and off-licence at the junction of Arundel Street and High Street West in about 1910.

Two

Buildings

The Howard Arms, Glossop, in 1903. Originally it was a farm and it was at this old inn that the stage coaches, travelling from Manchester, called to change horses and to offer food to the passengers and coachmen before they faced the long haul over the Snake Pass and the exposed moorland to Sheffield. The stables were round the back of the inn where fresh hay awaited the horses. Later, the inn extended its premises to include the building next door and today the entrance is not where the lady is standing, but at the other door with the half moon lintel.

This was the centre of Glossop, before the modern town had been developed, at the Old Market Cross, where the proclamations of the new monarchs were made. When Edward VII was proclaimed, a new cross was placed on the top of the shaft. The abbot and monks of Basingwerke Abbey were granted the lands in Glossopdale in 1157, by Henry II, for saving his life. The abbot established both a market and fair around the cross. This area is known as 'Old Glossop' whilst the modern Glossop developed further down the river where industrialisation was taking place.

CROSS AND CHURCH, GLOSSOP.

Another view of the Old Cross, reputedly built by the monks in 1290. All the buildings in this area are some of the oldest in Glossop. Glossop Parish Church can be seen in the background. The medieval market traders were advised to be fair and honest traders as they were selling their wares in the 'sight of God'. There has been a church on this site since 1157, when it was established by the Abbot of Basingwerke. Within this area were the old stocks, the pinfold and the 'lock-up'.

Church Street South, another part of the old town with a row of cottages which date from 1680. They belonged to the old yeomen farmers and were very handsome, built of grit stone with slate stone roofs, embellished by carved stone mullions and elegant chimney stacks. The large house at the top of the street was the home of the Bailiff of the Duke of Norfolk, who was very rich and powerful by local standards. Later it was occupied by the local butcher and he can be seen outside his door.

Tanyard Cottage on Mossy Lea, Old Glossop, overlooking the moors. It used to be occupied by Lord Howard's woodman.

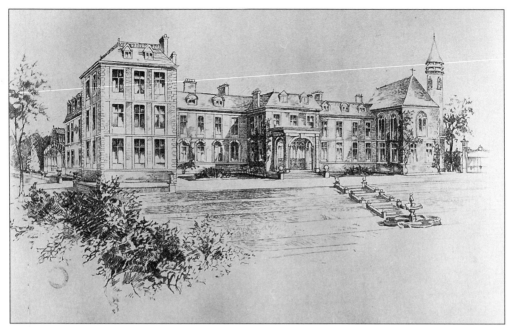

Glossop Hall, originally known as Royle Hall, was built in 1729 as a shooting lodge. The second hall was built and enlarged by the thirteenth Duke of Norfolk for his second son, Edward George Fitzalan Howard, the first Baron Howard of Glossop, who made it his home. His son Francis, second Baron Howard of Glossop, subsequently lived there too. Bernard Edward Howard, the third Baron, and father of the present Duke of Norfolk, sold the Glossopdale Estates after 300 years of Howard dominance in the dale and left Glossop to live in Yorkshire.

The Italian Gardens at the rear of the house as they appeared in 1906. The landscaped gardens became Manor Park in 1926 when the Howards left Glossop and Glossop Borough Council became responsible for the extensive lawns and gardens.

When the Howard family left Glossop Hall in 1925, the Howards sold up their estate in Glossop and it became Kingsmoor School, a private boarding school, which remained there until 1956 when the whole building was pulled down.

A photograph of the demolition of Glossop Hall, the stone of which was used to build an estate of bungalows on the same site. It is a sad picture as it marks the end of an era in the history of Glossop.

A photograph of Glossop Hall's lodge and gates. The lodge is still there today. The Hall can be seen in the background.

Howard Park gates with the park keeper's cottage and the swimming baths just behind. There used to be Sunday band concerts in the park in the late 1920s. A charming little girl poses for the photographer.

Partington Convalescent Home was built by Edward Partington (seen in the photograph), later Lord Doverdale, and given to Glossop Borough in 1908. It became a convalescent home for wounded soldiers in the First World War. Later it became Glossop Maternity Home and now it is privately owned.

A view of the front of the Partington Maternity Home, showing that it looked more like a country manor house than a hospital.

A view of central Glossop around 1910, with the large Wood's Mill complex at the back. Brownson's Corner is in the middle of the photograph, featuring the Jackson's Arcade with its glass colonnade. On the right is Finlay McKinley's chemist shop with the ducal crest over the door, awarded by the Duke of Norfolk. The two ladies on the left are attired in the uniform of the weavers of Glossop – clogs and shawl. Clogs were standard footwear then, like trainers today.

Glossop town centre in 1911, showing the tramlines down the main High Street amongst the cobblestones. At that time the corner shop with the dome was owned by Briggs, the newsagent. The street has no traffic except a horse and cart. The Town Hall, with its clock tower, was built by the twelfth Duke of Norfolk in 1836-37. The Victorian glass arcades over the shops are clearly seen on the left and on the right, over the Co-operative shopping emporium. Eventually they were removed and are now no longer to be seen.

Another view of Norfolk Square, showing the noble building on the right which used to house the Glossop Liberal Club, the foundation stone of which was laid by Sir Edward Partington, whose younger son, Oswald, was the Liberal MP for the High Peak constituency from 1900-1910. The building at the top of the square used to house the District Bank but now the Glossop Heritage Centre occupies the building and the District Bank moved into the bank building, which is now the National Westminster Bank.

Norfolk Square in the centre of Glossop in 1905, before the lawns and trees appeared. This open space was used for open public meetings. The bank in the centre has not yet been extended as it is today. The two tall chimneys belonged to the Howardtown Mill, owned by the Wood family. The dome in the middle of the photograph was built at the eastern end of the Town Hall complex in 1838 and for many years it housed Hawley's newsagent; before then it was always called Bradbury's Corner after the barber, Mr Bradbury. It was a favourite landmark in central Glossop but had to be demolished in 1937. The Midland Bank occupies the site today.

The Electric Palace, George Street, Glossop. The word 'electric' spoke volumes in the days of the early cinema. Electricity was looked on as the eighth wonder of the world; to enter a large hall, illuminated by electric lights and to watch moving pictures projected on a large screen by means of electricity, represented an escape from drab and unexciting surroundings for most people. The Palace first opened its doors in December 1911. The films shown were silent and the Palace was never fitted up for sound; it closed its doors in March 1931. Glossop Health Clinic now occupies the site of the old cinema.

The Empire cinema in High Street West was built in 1920 and first opened its doors in April 1921. The Empire offered a serious challenge to the Palace on George Street. In November 1929, the first 'talkie' was shown. The film was *Showboat*, with the music of Jerome Kern. Showing mainly films throughout the 1930s and 1940s, the Empire remained a popular place of entertainment for local people and queues stretched up and down the High Street and round the block when a popular film was featured. Despite the popularity of television the cinema lasted until 1963, when the building was demolished to make way for retail trade. In this view the cinema is decorated for the visit to Glossop of the first Cotton Queen.

The Whitfield Library was given to the people of Whitfield by Councillor George Ollerenshaw. He also built the houses on Wood Street and turned a previous eyesore into a 'pretty' street. The Reading Room's library was a handsome building containing a good selection of books.

Typical cottages of 1905, with their long sash windows and cotton blinds to pull down at night. These were in High Street West, Glossop, and were demolished to make way for the Mobil garage.

Simmondley Village, a lovely little hamlet on the outskirts of Glossop, as it looked in the 1930s. It consisted of a few cottages, set around the village green, with a seventeenth century manor house and its village pub with its scrubbed floors. The lanes passing through the village were quiet, country ways with the odd horse and cart rumbling through.

Simmondley Hall, the old manor house, no doubt built on the site of a previous timbered hall. In 1579 the present building was built. The hall used to be occupied by one of the Hadfield family, who built Hadfield Hall.

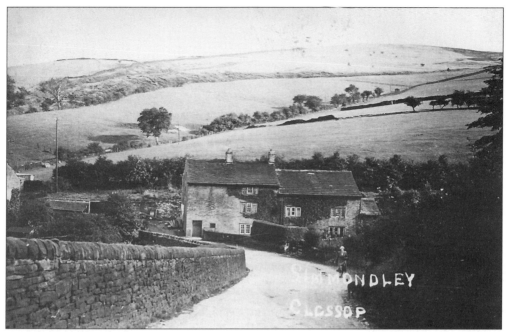

Another view of Simmondley with an old weaver's cottage in the middle. On the ground floor the women and children would be occupied spinning the raw cotton and the man of the house would be weaving on the top floor. Living accommodation was on the middle floor.

A view showing the charm of the old cottages of Simmondley gathered around the green. Today the village has attracted a large amount of house building which has somewhat altered the original appearance of the old hamlet.

A panoramic view of Glossop in the 1950s, taken from the rooftop of Howardtown Mill in High Street East. It was the largest mill in Glossop but now all the buildings in the foreground have been demolished. Most of the other mill chimneys in the background have disappeared and the air quality has greatly improved.

The road from Glossop goes southward out of the town. The moorland which surrounds the town can be clearly seen. The mill in the middle housed John Walton's Bleach Works until 1950, when it moved into other accommodation, finally closing in the 1970s.

Some of the past hot summers bred thunderstorms up in the hills and turned gentle streams into raging torrents which often flooded the town. Here at the Junction Inn, where two streams meet, the water used to overflow onto the main road into Glossop. Customers at the nearby Co-op found shopping rather difficult on this day in 1944.

This mill was one of the big ones in Padfield. It belonged to Herbert Rhodes and it was always referred to as Rhodes Top Mill. It operated its own little railway which brought in the coal to power the mill.

Another view of Padfield, within the Glossop boundary. The brook running through the village attracted the building of mills which employed most of the inhabitants of the small community. On the left of the photograph is the other side of Rhodes Mill.

The Spinners Arms in Hadfield, when it was just an ale house. In the foreground was a row of very old houses with a Dickensian flavour, with small mullion windows and steps at the rear leading to the upper rooms. They were demolished at the beginning of this century and today a landscaped garden occupies the site.

Another view of Hadfield, with Hadfield Road, in 1908. The top house was one of the oldest buildings in the area, with its small windows and its stone slab roof. The lady on the right and the boys are wearing clogs, worn by most people at that time.

The area around the Hadfield Old Hall, where the seventeenth century hall was opposite this old farm house. People used to go to the farm to buy their milk and carried it home in big stone jugs.

An aerial view of Glossop showing it surrounded by high moorlands, with the High Street passing through the centre of town. In the foreground is the large Wren Nest Mill, the second largest cotton mill in Glossop, which closed in the mid-1950s; apart from a few small businesses, the building has remained empty ever since. Most of the building was demolished to make way for a large supermarket and in 1996 a large fire destroyed quite a lot of the main building. The tall mill chimney of Howardtown Mill can be seen on the extreme right. The Duke of Norfolk built the railway line into Glossop from the main Manchester–Sheffield line, which by-passed the town. He built the railway to save the Glossop mills from decline by giving the town a direct link with Manchester.

Three

Transport

An early form of transport - a landau around 1910.

The Glossop horse ambulance in 1906.

The Royal Mail travelled in such a vehicle in 1906.

Horse and carriage in High Street East, Glossop, outside Mr Hamnett's jewellers shop. Miss Hamnett is on the left. Mr Hamnett was a well known reporter, writing a weekly column on Glossop history, of which he was an authority.

A pony trap on Glossop market ground. At the turn of the century travel was a little less frenetic than it is today.

Motorman John Byron, with the Demi Car belonging to Glossop Tramways. This car only ran from the town centre up to 'John Wood's gates', the entrance to Whitfield House, home of John Wood, the eldest Wood brother of the Wood's Mill complex.

Another view of Norfolk Square in 1904, with Bradbury's dome in the centre. The three trams in the photograph show that a regular service was available to the people of Glossop - or was it like today, when one bus arrives, and then another two arrive at the same time? The toll bar weigh house behind the dome was demolished to make way for the new post office, built in 1923.

In 1903 Glossop Tramways appeared with four and a half miles of single track with termini at Hadfield Station and the Queens Arms. The tram is shown at Old Glossop outside the Queens. The ladies on the top would have to hold onto their hats.

Glossop Tramways Company was too small to make it viable and it closed down in 1927 to be replaced by the early buses. One is seen here, travelling along Brookfield on its way into Glossop in the late 1920s.

A steam tractor pulling a string of wagons carrying bales of cotton cloth from the weaving sheds of the Glossop mills, up to the John Walton's Bleach Works at Charlestown Road, just up the road from the Drovers' Arms inn on the photograph.

Glossop signal box, just outside Glossop Station in 1889, with an old steam locomotive waiting on the tracks.

The well known 'Tiger' tractor, photographed in Norfolk Street, Glossop, having just been loaded at Glossop railway station with logs destined for the Olive & Partington paper mill at Charlestown Road. These tractors rumbled up and down Victoria Street every day.

A very unusual railway built by the Waterside Cotton Mill Company for the sole purpose of carrying freight from the marshalling yard at Gamesley to the mill at Hadfield. It had to cross two level crossings, one at Gamesley and one near the Pear Tree Inn at Hadfield, and it crossed over the main road into Glossop near Woolley Bridge. The train shown here has just crossed this bridge and is travelling over the raised gantry passing behind Brookfield.

The Snake Inn on the Snake Pass, with a very early motor car. The inn was built by the Duke of Devonshire, whose coat of arms features a serpent, after which the Snake Inn and the Pass got their name.

We're off on a day trip, wearing our holiday clothes, in an early charabanc in the early 1930s.

Another view of the centre of Glossop with an early motor car travelling down High Street West. The small white building in the middle of the photograph is intriguing; on the outside is a notice saying 'Fire Telephone'. One can also see the drinking fountain, erected by Mrs John Wood of Whitfield House. It is still there today as a feature of Norfolk Square.

A railway goods wagon belonging to the London & North Eastern Railway, pictured outside a Glossop railway warehouse, which now houses a large supermarket.

The railway from Manchester to Sheffield had to negotiate two high viaducts over two river gorges. This one was at Broadbottom. Originally built of wood, box girders later replaced the wooden arches to support the heavy freight wagons which were much heavier than the train in the picture.

Another view of the Broadbottom viaduct which was built in 1842 over the River Etherow, a tributary of the River Mersey. The original symmetry was ruined later when extra brick piers had to be built between the stone supports to support the heavy coal trains. The road bridge over the river is in the foreground, built to carry horses and carts, but today double decked buses negotiate this narrow bridge.

Dinting Arches, built in 1844, four miles to the east of Broadbottom Arches. Again the early structure was made of wood, later replaced by the iron structure and the extra brick supports. This early station was called Glossop Station, as the town had been by-passed by the main railway line. The thirteenth Duke of Norfolk built the branch line to Glossop from Dinting at his own expense in 1847. He also built Glossop Station; the station in the picture became Dinting Station.

A view of Dinting Arches, showing the men building the extra brick supports between the stone piers. The arches to the left are still open; they were bricked up later to strengthen the arches to support the heavy trains, which used to have as many as thirty wagons, carrying coal from Yorkshire to Lancashire. The river can be seen in the foreground and Dinting Print Works is clearly visible through the viaduct.

The switching on of the new traffic lights in the centre of Glossop in 1938. Constable Walter Thornley had been on traffic duty at the cross-roads longer than any other officer and he was chosen to switch on the lights. Present at the ceremony were Cllr J. Hague, Mayor of Glossop, Cllr J.R.A. Beckman, Deputy Mayor and Chair of the Watch Committee, Mr S. Fletcher (County Council), Alderman G. Wharmby, Mr F. Ivinson (County Surveyor), Mr W.S.A. Robinson (Town Clerk), Mr G. Faulds (Borough Surveyor) and Mr R.C. Greensmith (Chief Constable).

Four
Working Life

Wren Nest Mill, the second largest mill in Glossop, was built by Matthew Ellison, the Howard agent in 1815. His step nephew, Francis Sumner, managed the mill and locally it was always called Sumner's Mill.

Inside a weaving shed in a local Glossop mill. The noise was horrendous and most weavers became deaf and were expert lip readers. The rows of deafening, clattering looms were terrifying. The women looked after four or more looms in an atmosphere filled with cotton lint and went home covered in it.

The weaving shed at Shepley Mill, Brookfield, Glossop. The decorations are possibly to celebrate the coronation of King George V in 1911.

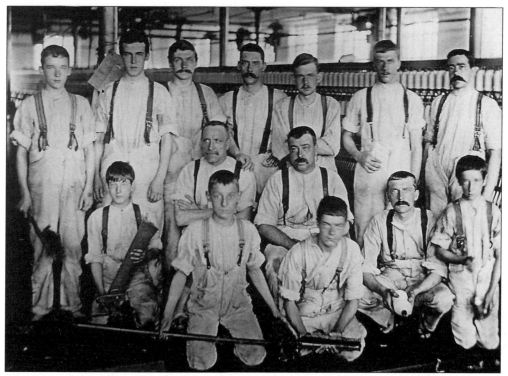

The spinners at a Glossop mill, showing how young some of them were. Because of the high humidity, which was necessary to prevent the breakage of the cotton, the men had to work barefoot and wore very thin cotton shirts and trousers.

The Wharf, or Shepley Street, at Old Glossop, with the old Shepley Mill on the left, situated by one of the moorland streams which powered the early mills of Glossop. Every stream had a cluster of mills on it.

The Manchester Ship Canal, built to bring the raw cotton imported from America into the heart of Manchester, was formally opened by Queen Victoria on 21 May 1884.

Glossop mill owners bought their raw cotton in Manchester. The first cotton ship docked on 17 January 1894 with 4,170 bales of cotton.

The *Enchantress* leaving Trafford Wharf at the ceremonial opening of the Ship Canal by Queen Victoria. Transport on the canal made the raw cotton much cheaper than when it had been channelled through Liverpool first.

Built in 1790, Gnat Hole Mill, belonging to the Robinson family, was one of the oldest woollen mills in Glossop. This mill continued in wool even when the great cotton mills were springing up all over Glossop.

Railway men at Hadfield. The 'G.C.' on the railway wagons refers to Glossop Central, the original name of Glossop Station.

Some of the inmates of Glossop Workhouse around 1880. The workhouse was built in 1840 to house the poor people of Glossop, and was extended in 1895. Being sent to the workhouse carried great social stigma and the harsh, stern discipline caused a great deal of suffering. Some of the faces reflect this in the photograph. Today it is Shire Hill Hospital, owned by the local health authority and has a totally different atmosphere.

A group of carters from the John Walton's Bleach Works at Turn Lea, photographed outside the Drovers' Arms inn when Albert Buckley Taylor was the landlord.

Leisurely selling from the horse and carts in Lambgates, Hadfield, around 1910. The fish merchant in his clogs is very popular with the local cat population and behind him, the greengrocer is weighing out his apples.

'Firewood Sam' in Salisbury Street, Hadfield, with his axe in his hand and the firewood in his barrow. He was a well known figure when every house had an open fire.

The *Glossop Chronicle* staff in 1910. Back row, left to right: Vic Connor (reporter), Sam Sidebottom (reporter), Jack Charlesworth (compositor), Sam Bealey (manager), Ivan Sharp (reporter), Mr Bealey jnr (apprentice). Front row: George Turner (accountant), Frank Booth (compositor), Levi Baran (printer), Mr Higginbottom (printer), Leonard Clarke (apprentice), later killed in the First World War.

The staff at Glossop's cinema, the Empire, which was opened in 1921 and closed in 1963. At the time of the photograph the manager was Mr S.A. Jones, with some of his long serving staff. Mr Mark Schofield was the projectionist for thirty-seven years and showed 2,000 films to the happy cinema-goers of Glossop. Minnie Yates served for thirty-six years, Gladys Hobson for thirty-four years, Alice Hobson for twenty years and Isaac Riley for twelve years: a wonderful record. The usherettes and attendants were Doreen Bradshaw, Ada Allsop, Kathleen Zastawney, Maria Morrison, Bridget Hall, Kenneth Higgs and Keith Cooper.

Members of the Working Men's Club at Woolley Bridge, Hadfield. The number of buttonholes and bowler hats suggests it must have been a big occasion.

The members of the Glossop Fire Brigade - who also served in the Police Force - with their shiny new fire engine in 1900, which was pulled by horses on loan from Glossop Carriage Company. The members are seen with some Hadfield 'worthies'. Front row, left to right: Mr Cooper (police), Mr Greaves (baker), Mr Martin (draper), Mr Braddock (grocer), Mr Thornley (mill manager), Mr Dawson (decorator), Mr Israel Warrington (overlooker).

72

Glossop Police Force was formed in 1867. The photograph shows the Force around 1899 when John Gregory Hodgson was Chief Constable. He also served as Superintendent of Glossop Fire Brigade from 1905-1921 alongside his men, who acted as firemen.

The blacksmith's shop in Manor Street, Glossop, owned by Boardman and Sons, later known as Nield's, where Wilfred Hall, Glossop's oldest blacksmith, worked. The blacksmith's shop was a vital service in the days of horse drawn transport.

Dinting Print Works staff on a day's outing around 1919. One man seems to be wearing his soldier's uniform; perhaps he served in the First World War. Flat caps have been exchanged for bowlers, trilbys and straw hats.

Dinting Print Works. In 1852 Edmund Potter, grandfather of the famous Beatrix, commenced the print works with his cousin, Charles, at Dinting Vale, Glossop. It grew to be one of the largest print works in Europe. Edmund died in 1883. The works became a limited company and weathered the vagaries of the cotton industry, but eventually closed in 1966.

Isaac Jackson was another local industrialist, who bought the Town Hall from the Duke of Norfolk and presented it to the Borough of Glossop. His factory was in Old Glossop. The photograph shows the factory when munitions were manufactured for the First World War.

The staff at Glossop Post Office, photographed outside the new post office building, constructed in 1923 in Victoria Street.

An aerial view over Glossop with Charlestown Road on the right, leading to the large paper
mill of Olive & Partington in the centre of the photograph. In the distance Wren Nest Mill on
the left, and Howardtown Mill on the right, are clearly visible. Whitfield House, home of Sir
John Hill-Wood, is evident middle right, set in its wooded grounds.

Five

The Wood Family

This silver casket was presented to Mrs Anne Kershaw Wood by the Borough of Glossop when she became the first Lady Freeman of the Borough. The decoration on the casket included the Borough Coat of Arms, plus enamelled paintings of Howard Park and Wood's Hospital.

Mrs Anne Kershaw Wood was Glossop's first Lady Freeman as she was one of Glossop's greatest benefactors. She was born on 1 January 1838 and married Samuel Wood JP in 1869, a member of the firm John Wood Bros., the largest cotton manufacturers in Glossop.

Mr Samuel Wood (1819-1888) third son of John Wood, the founder of the Howardtown Cotton Mill. He is seen with his son, Samuel Hill-Wood (1872-1949).

Whitfield Church Sermons Parade in Victoria Street in 1904 with Anne Kershaw Wood in the centre. Usually 1,000 people attended the Sunday School Sermons when the Whitfield Band led the parade. Sermons Parades were the highlight of the year, an occasion for processions and new clothes, the one being the chance to show off the other. The ladies' decorated hats and the frills and flounces were the highest fashion of the day.

Mrs Anne Kershaw Wood at a tree planting ceremony outside Whitfield Infant School in Victoria Street. The school was built in 1913 by her son, Sir Samuel Hill-Wood, who later became the MP for the High Peak constituency from 1910-1929. In 1943 the infant school became Whitfield Wartime Nursery to help working mothers, and is still used by youngsters today.

Moorfield House, home of Daniel Wood and Samuel Wood and his wife Anne Kershaw Wood. After the Wood family departed, the house was used as a seminary for Catholic priests; later a fire almost ruined the house. Today it is divided into two dwellings.

Moorfield became a convalescent home for wounded soldiers of the First World War. A group of them are shown at the lodge gates and the house can be seen through the trees.

It was not as a baronet that Sir Samuel Hill-Wood was remembered, but as 'Young Sam', upon whom devolved the leadership of the Conservatives and the Church of England in Glossop. He was MP for the High Peak constituency from 1910-1929, but he drew further away from Glossop to live in London. He was a Derbyshire County Cricketer and so were his sons. He also took the Glossop Football Team into the First Division of the League, if only for one year, but they remained in the Second Division for fifteen seasons. He was also President of Glossop Cricket League for over fifty years and after his retirement, he became Chairman of the Arsenal Football Club. He died in 1949 and was buried at Whitfield Church, alongside his parents.

Sir Samuel Hill-Wood married the Hon Anne Selina Decima Bateman-Hanbury, second daughter of the second Baron Bateman, in 1899, and they had four sons: Sir Basil Hill-Wood, Wilfred Hill-Wood CBE, Dennis John Charles Hill-Wood MC and Charles Kerrison Hill-Wood. Two of the sons succeeded their father as Chairman of the Arsenal Football Club and a Hill-Wood is chairman of the club today.

Sir John Hill-Wood (1857-1927). He was a cousin of Sir Samuel Hill-Wood and married Gertrude Emily Bateman-Hanbury, third daughter of the second Baron Bateman and younger sister of Sir Samuel's wife. They lived at Whitfield House, Glossop, and later moved to Hengrave Hall, Bury St Edmunds. Like his cousin he did not work in the mill but chose politics, becoming MP for Stalybridge from 1910-1922. They had only one son who succeeded his father as MP for Stalybridge and Hyde from 1924-1929.

Gertrude Emily Bateman, second wife of Sir John Hill-Wood, built three drinking fountains in Glossop, one in Norfolk Square, one in Victoria Street and one in Manor Park Road. The fountains catered for people's thirst by providing a cup and a tap, a drinking trough for the horses and one lower down for the dogs. The only one left today is in Norfolk Square; the one in Victoria Street was demolished and the one in Manor Park Road was removed to Hengrave Hall.

This photograph illustrates the beauty of Howard Park, showing the lake, Wood's Hospital and the Wood Memorial. The trees and lawns were set out at the personal expense of Anne Kershaw Wood. Originally it was called Victoria Park to commemorate the Jubilee of Queen Victoria, but then its name was changed to Howard Park in gratitude to the Duke of Norfolk, who gave the ground to Mrs Wood.

The Wood Memorial was built by Mrs Anne Kershaw Wood, symbolising the town's dependence on cotton. It features a weaver sitting on a bale of cotton with drinking fountains on two sides and the heads of her husband Samuel, and his brother, Daniel, in bas relief on the other two sides. Samuel and Daniel both died in the year that the park opened.

Woods Monument, Glossop Park.

Another view of the Wood Memorial monument in Howard Park within its beautiful setting of elegant lawns and rare trees, planted at a cost of £6,000.

The swimming baths were built in Howard Park in the Jubilee Year of 1887. As well as the Victorian swimming baths, slipper baths and Turkish baths were available as an alternative to the tin baths in front of the fire. These were constructed at the personal expense of Anne Kershaw Wood and her husband. Wood's Hospital was built in the same park in the same year.

The Sermons Parade of Whitfield Church in High Street, Glossop in 1904, led by the vicar, William Martin-Ellis and Mr Samuel Hill-Wood. The Sermons Parades used to take place in spring or summer to celebrate the founding of the Sunday Schools.

The impressive gates at the entrance to Moorfield House, with a very old motor car leaving the house and its extensive wooded grounds in the background in about 1919.

The Wood family vault, built in 1914 at St James's Church, Whitfield. The builders on the right of the photograph were Mr Goddard's men. Mr Goddard, with the beard, is on the right of the front row.

An aerial view of the largest mill in Glossop. Howardtown Mill was owned by the Wood family. It grew to be one of the largest mills in Europe where both spinning and weaving took place and it employed more Glossop cotton workers than any other mill in the district. Today there is very little left of the building, most of it being demolished after 1956 when it closed forever.

Six
Churches and Chapels

All Saints' Parish Church in 1849. A church on this site goes back to Norman times.

The original church of St James, Whitfield, built in 1846. The parish originally included the entire townships of Hadfield, Dinting and Chunal and parts of Whitfield, Padfield and Glossop. After the consecration of the church, the Sunday School was held in its gallery until the schools were completed in 1848.

Whitfield Church had a chancel much shorter than the present one; the gallery ran down both sides. A new chancel was built with an apse in 1896. In 1925, Sir John Wood built the memorial chapel. Members of the Wood family erected most of the stained glass windows in the church in memory of various relatives.

Whitfield Parish Hall choir, *c.* 1928. Back row, left to right: Arthur Millward, Arthur Chambers, Albert Millward, Asa Moreton, George Wild, Francis Metcalfe. Front row: Alice Rowbottom, -?-, -?-, Alice Hinchcliffe, -?-, Revd H.V. Nichol-Griffith (vicar), Eli Hadfield, (lay reader), Alice Higginbottom, Mary Sidebottom, -?-, -?-. The Revd H.V. Nichol-Griffith was the vicar from 1926-1934.

Whitfield Parish Hall, opened in 1908, was in Kershaw Street. Whitfield Church owned many buildings in well populated areas of the town and its parishioners could meet and worship near their homes. Although the parish hall was little more than a corrugated iron structure, the interior was tastefully and respectfully decorated, with its hand crocheted altar cloth and stained glass window.

Whitfield bell ringers in 1928. Hand bell ringing was a popular pastime in Glossop and most of the church bell ringers had a team of hand bell ringers, who often used to give concerts.

Whitfield Church Sermons Parade in 1904, with the ladies of Whitfield on show in their new hats and wonderful Edwardian fashions. The milliners shops must have worked overtime to make these individual creations.

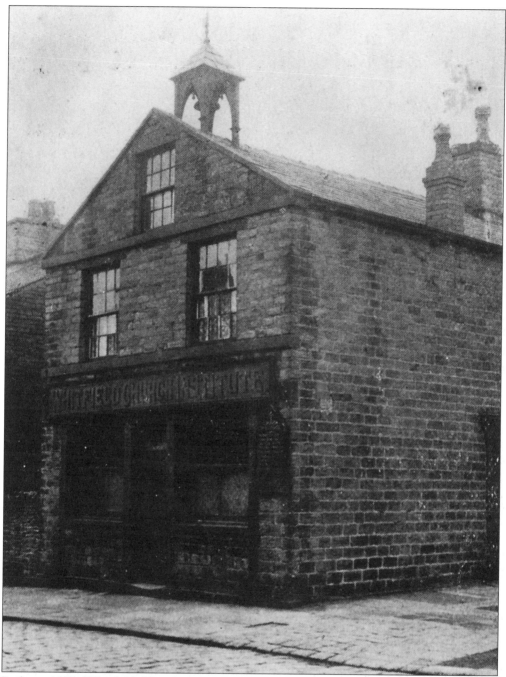

Built in 1908, Whitfield Church Institute used to be situated on Chapel Street. This was another building belonging to Whitfield Church. Originally it was situated on George Street and was known as George Street Mission, but then it moved to Chapel Street to the Volunteer Inn.

Littlemoor Independent Chapel opened in 1811 in Victoria Street. The large Wood's Mill complex is at the bottom of the hill, its chimneys dominating the skyline. The Sunday School next door was one of the first Day Schools in Glossop.

Another view of the Littlemoor Chapel, showing the Gladstone Street entrance with the cobblestones. The chapel was surrounded by its own graveyard.

Glossop used to have its own Salvation Army Band.

Glossop Mission Band, photographed outside the Mission in Ellison Street, with Pastor Howton, a well known figure in Glossop at the beginning of the century. He used to lead his 'sheep' to the top of the Nab overlooking Glossop, and lead an open air service of worship. He was outstanding in his bright blue flowing robes so could be seen by everyone.

Adam Pyle Hamilton Wilson (1889-1906), Vicar of All Saints' Parish Church. He was the first vicar to introduce vestments. During his ministry he saw new choir stalls and a new fauld stool, the gift of Daniel Wood, a new font, a gift from Charles Knowles, husband of the eldest daughter of Lord Doverdale, and a wrought iron chancel screen.

Charles Dudley Hart (1908-1917), Vicar of All Saints' Parish Church. He saw the new nave started in 1914 and wanted a design more medieval than early nineteenth century, with hexagonal piers. These piers were built with Mouselow stone from the local quarry.

Zion School, Simmondley Lane, in 1905. The school building was an extension to that of the chapel.

Pupils at St Andrew's School, built in Railway Street, Hadfield, in 1905. Mrs Hutchinson was the headteacher and Miss Wilde, the class teacher.

Dinting Church School in 1899, with the headmaster, Mr Lawton.

Hague Street School in Whitfield was not attached to a place of worship but it was built by Joseph Hague, a self-made millionaire, in 1778, before the denominational schools were built. Pupils had to pay for their education and the money helped to pay the wages of the headmaster. In 1881 W.P. Evason was the headmaster, when fees were 10s 6d per quarter, until the school was closed in 1925 due to free education being offered in other schools.

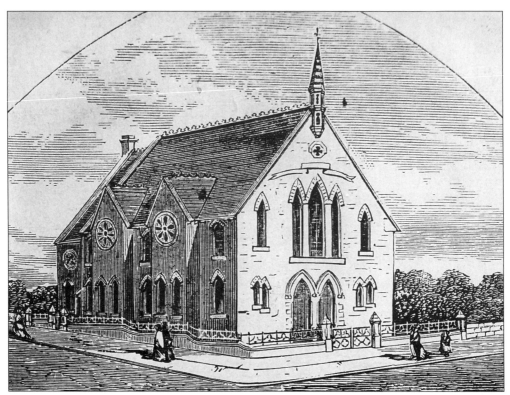

Mount Pleasant Church in St Marys Road, built in 1868. The Sunday School was built alongside in 1875. The original services were held in a room in Charles Street when there were twenty-three members; then the services were held in the Temperance Hall (later the Labour Club) in Chapel Street. Ten years later they built the present church.

All Saints' Catholic Church. Around 1800, a private chapel was built in the grounds of Glossop Hall, the basis of the Roman Catholic parish of All Saints. When numbers grew, the twelfth Duke of Norfolk built the church at his own expense on a site near to Glossop Hall. The Howard family embellished the inside and outside of the church with unfailing generosity until they left Glossop.

A view of Norfolk Square in 1926, with the Roman Catholic procession culminating in a service in the square. The new building in the background was the Liberal Club. Sir Edward Partington laid the foundation stone in 1914. The original building next to the Liberal Club used to be a funeral parlour but that has now been incorporated into the nearby bank, which stands there today.

A similar view of Norfolk Square but one of the early buses can be seen in front of the Norfolk Arms. The tall chimneys in the background belonged to the great Wood's Mill and dominated the town.

Charlesworth Top Chapel, in 1920. The original chapel was reputedly built by the monks who owned the land in Glossopdale in 1154. These monks used to pass between their monastery in North Wales and their lands in Derbyshire and would need a place to rest and shelter on this wild and dangerous ridge, as well as a place of worship. The old mountain road is still known as Monks Road. The building was pulled down and replaced in the nineteenth century and there is no other instance in England of a parochial church or chapel remaining in Non-Conformist hands for over 300 years.

Charlesworth St John's School, *c.* 1905.

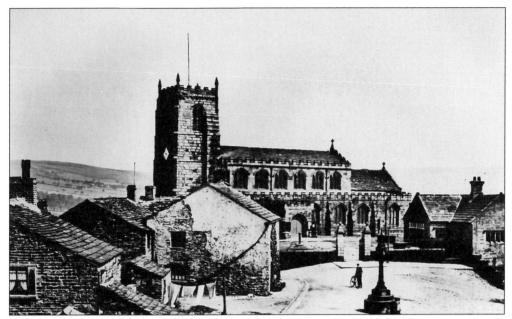

Mottram Church on top of the hill can be seen from all over Glossopdale. There was a church on the site in Norman times.

The bell ringers at Mottram Church after ringing a record peel of 16,680 changes in nine hours and forty minutes in 1906. Included in the photograph are Isaac Sidebottom, Joseph Goddard, Samuel Stott, Charles Marsland and Frank Hall.

Dinting Holy Trinity Church, which stands by the old turnpike road into Glossop. Today it is surrounded by trees and lawns which soften its appearance. The church was built through the generosity of Daniel, Samuel and Anne Kershaw Wood; the tower and spire were paid for by John Wood and Miss Wood. The church was consecrated in 1875.

Seven
Leisure Activities

Glossop Ladies' Swimming Club, *c.* 1902.

Glossop Cricket Club pavilion in 1920. Alf Charlesworth is on the left, with Charles Olliviere and Alf Berwick.

Glossop Cricket Team in 1903, the winners of the Central Lancashire League. Back row from left to right: E. Collier (secretary), A. Morton, C. Hunter, J.T. Booth, L.F. Ward, A. Wild (scorer). Middle row: S. Cadman, A. Charlesworth, Samuel Hill-Wood, W.F. Dalton, I. Dearnley. Front row: J. Bowden, A. Berwick, C.A. Olliviere. The captain, Samuel Hill-Wood, brought over C.A. Olliviere from the West Indies as a professional player, one of the first players to come from there to play in this country.

Glossop Football Team, 1904. Back row from left to right: A. Berwick (trainer), Synot, Davis, Orr, J.P. Sutcliffe (secretary). Middle row: Phillips, Gall, Cairns, A. Goodall, Murphy, Lawrence. Front row: Brown, Boden, Maginnis.

Glossop Football Team in 1913/14.

Glossop Concertina Band. Mr Bowden, with the baton in his hand, was the leader. Young George Bowden is on his left. When George grew up he had his own band, The Regent, which played at all the dances in Glossop.

Glossop Police Force Football Team in 1920. Back row from left to right: Sam Roe, Sam Wedgewood, Sam Dutton, Stonewall Jackson, Walter Marsden. Front row: Fred Bradbury, Walter Thornley, Able Garlick, Albert Isaacs, Leo Birt. At the front is Arnold Jackson.

Glossop Traders' Football Team, c. 1914. They seemed to wear a very strange strip in those days, and a question could be asked about the strange patriotic outfit of the gentleman in the middle of the back row.

Isaac Jackson's Football Team from Hawkshead Factory in 1913/14.

Hadfield St Andrew's Junior Football Team in 1919. At the back is the Revd A.C.M. White with Jim Wood (secretary). Back row from left to right: Horace Wood, Tom Renshaw (captain), Harold Warhurst, Jack Hallam. Middle row: Bill Chatterton, Charlie Bamford, Ernest Thompson. Front row: Harold Jones, Tom Peel, George Crook, Albert Lawton, Sam Jones.

St Luke's Amateur Football Team in 1911/12.

Dinting Cricket Club. Arthur Knott was captain. Back row from left to right: Knott, Brookes, Jones, Kirk, Orr. Middle row: Ford, Booth, Richardson, Sheppard, Coxon. Front row: Appleton, Fielding, Salmon.

Zion Chapel Cricket Team in 1924. Whole families were involved in Sunday School activities. Most Sunday Schools had football teams and cricket teams. In the photograph are three Sidebottom brothers and their father, and also two Jackson brothers.

Old Glossop Morris Dancers, 1925. Back row from left to right: W. Brooks, H. Norbury, F. Colclough, J. Brothwell, -?-, W. Dix, H. Walsh, T. Eyre, R. Blackwell, S.W. Hall. Middle row: W. Winterbottom, W. Bowden, J. Priestley, G. Frane, E. Norbury, E. Lawton, J. Mottram, F. Smith, T. Byron, G. Thornhill. Front row: L. Dix, C. Downs, W. Dewsnap, F. Connor.

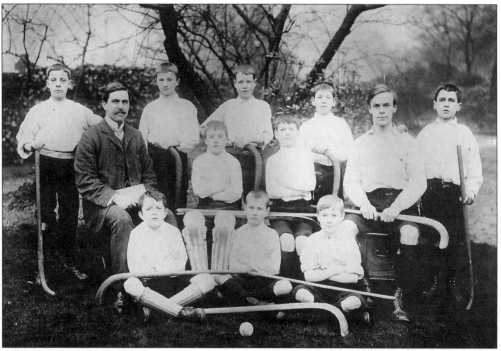

Whitfield School Hockey Team, 1904. Major Morris, headmaster of the school from 1895-1930, appears to be very proud of his hockey team, which was probably trained by Mr Lewis.

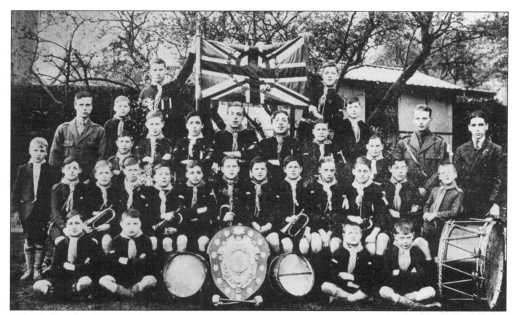

Whitfield Parish Church Boy Scouts, 1928. President and scout master Eric Bowden, in uniform, is on the right of the back row. On the left of the same row is Mr H. Lomas, the treasurer.

The Girl Guides at Whitfield Church in 1928, with the vicar, the Revd H.V. Nicoll-Griffith.

The opening of St Mary's Sports Club. Lord Doverdale is in the centre with his daughter-in-law, Mrs Herbert Partington, on his left.

Littlemoor Operatic Company was famous for its musical productions in the 1930s. Two stalwarts of the company were Miss Cissie Sidebottom and Mr Arthur Bridge. In this photograph they can be seen with the full company in *The Desert Song*. Arthur Bridge was the famous Red Shadow.

114

Eight

Events
and Celebrations

A decorated float in Glossop Carnival Parade in the 1930s, passing through High Street West.

Whitfield Well Dressing in 1920, with the high decorated arch over Whitfield Cross near to the well. Alderman Dick Sellars was the mayor and can be seen with the members of the Well Dressing Committee.

The arch again, with the Rush Cart. This was a solid four-square pyramid of rushes, bundled into sheaves and the four sides trimmed, the whole being decorated with flowers. The Rush Cart was processed around the streets of Whitfield. When they reached the church, the cart was stripped and the rushes were strewn on its flagged floor to keep the feet of the worshippers warm during the cold and snowy winter.

The Morris Dancers and Concertina Band players at the decorated well. The Whitfield Well was decorated every year and the money raised at the celebrations went into a 'clog fund' to buy clogs for the poor people of Glossop and to help the Wood's Hospital.

Mrs Mary Alice Partington MBE JP, was married to Herbert Partington, elder son of Lord Doverdale. She lived at Talbot House and worked incessantly to raise money for Wood's Hospital and Partington Home. In the early days of the century she worked tirelessly for the Liberal cause in the High Peak area. When her husband died in his mayoral year, she was invited to take over the office although she was not an elected member of the Borough Council.

Sir Edward Partington, later Lord Doverdale, and his daughter-in-law, Mary Alice Partington, planting trees in Howard Park.

The opening of the Convalescent Home in North Road in 1908. The grand motor car probably belonged to Sir Edward Partington, who built the home. Mary Alice Partington, his daughter-in-law, was instrumental in changing the Convalescent Home to the Maternity Hospital in 1920.

Sir Edward Partington and his daughter-in-law lead a procession from Howard Street Chapel along Howard Street. The chapel has been demolished and the adjacent Sunday School is now a doctor's surgery.

Members of Glossop Police Force leading a parade, followed by Sir Edward Partington and the Mayor of Glossop, William Jackson, in 1925.

The Proclamation of King George V in Glossop. This was the first proclamation not announced at the Old Cross in Old Glossop but outside the Town Hall, in the centre of Glossop. The mayor, Brooke Furniss, can be seen with other aldermen and councillors at this ceremony in 1910.

A view of Norfolk Square at the ceremony celebrating the coronation of King George V in 1911. The Co-operative store on the left was then graced with a glass colonnade. Norfolk Square was at that time a rough piece of land where all public meetings took place. The buildings at the top of the Square remain little changed today.

A body of ex-servicemen, wearing their medals proudly outside the Glossop Drill Hall. Enrolment posters are clearly visible. The Drill Hall later became part of the Market Hall.

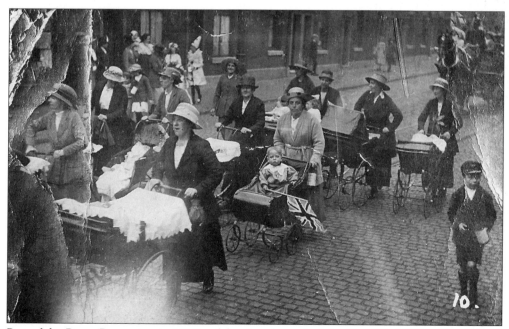

Part of the Peace Procession in 1919, celebrating the end of the First World War. The fashion of pramware has changed a little since then!

Whitfield Well Dressing Parade in 1920, with the Morris Men, boys and girls dancing outside the Roebuck Inn, as part of the Well Dressing celebrations.

Glossop Market ground with the old Theatre Royal in the background. An ox is being roasted and the hungry children are waiting patiently. The clogs and shawls on the two youngsters in the foreground illustrate that children always copied their parents in their choice of clothes.

The Old Market Cross in Old Glossop in 1927, beautifully decorated for the Rose Queen Festival, maybe at the Dressing of the Well in Old Glossop.

In 1911 the coronation of King George V was commemorated in Howard Park by displaying a floral clock, planted by the gardeners, seen here posing for the photographer. Mr J. Malkin was the Mayor of Glossop in that year.

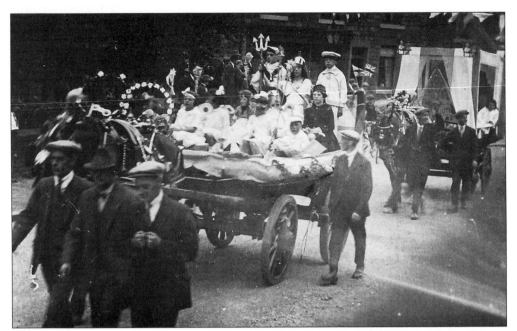

Hadfield Carnival in Queen Street, Hadfield, in the 1930s. Front left are the three Cheven brothers, coal merchants, who used to win many top prizes for their decorated horses with gleaming horse brasses. The money raised at the carnival was given to Wood's Hospital and eventually enough was raised to provide the X-ray equipment there.

Another decorated float in Glossop Carnival Parade. This cart belonged to the Co-op and the horse would pull it around the town every day. However, on carnival day its hooves were polished and painted and its body decorated with flowers and gleaming brasses.

Peck's greengrocers used their new motor lorry in the carnival. They even painted its tyres and polished their fruit.

The carnival parade wending its way up Victoria Street in 1920. Francis Sumner lent one of his early lorries to be used to carry men dressed up from Belle Vue Gardens in Manchester.

The year 1920 saw the Glossop Carnival finishing in Manor Park for the first time. The photograph shows members of the Red Cross Society in the park, resting after the parade.

Members of the Glossop branch of the Red Cross and behind them are the Boy Scouts in procession in Glossop Road, Gamesly, around 1920. A very early motor car can be seen on the right.

Glossop soldiers at camp in North Wales in 1910. Back row from left to right: Needham, Jones and Patchett. Front row: Marsden, Harrop, Matthews.

Mrs Platt, wife of Edward Platt of Station Mill, Hadfield (later Wilmans) with a crowd of ladies at one of her famous garden parties, this one at Mersey Bank House to celebrate the coronation of King George V in June 1911.

The unveiling of the Glossop Cenotaph in March 1922, erected to honour the dead of the First World War. Francis Howard, second Baron of Glossop, performed the unveiling ceremony and the Revd Martin Ellis, of Whitfield Church, led the dedication service.